MY FIRST BEST FRIEND

By Derrick Washington

"Everyone dreams of creating something special. Karter, Kennedy, and Keaton, you all are my something special and I cant wait to show your gifts to the world."

From the first time the nurse placed you in my arms,
I knew we would forever have an unbreakable bond.

Every time I look at you, I see me—
the man you'll look to for guidance above all others you meet.

When you were a baby, I watched you for hours,
eagerly awaiting your first step, first words,
and the day you and I could play.
Even to this day, things you do still have me amazed.

From the first time you said, "Dada," I knew in my heart
that my best friend and I would never be apart.

Watching closely as you took your first step,
I could see your independence, a little boy with so much pep.

In those early days, though you tripped, tumbled, and fell,
From your determination I knew in my heart you would do well.

Teaching you to catch, play ball, and build castles in the sand,
I enjoyed making memories with my best friend.

You felt that there was nothing you couldn't do,
and like any good daddy, I told you this was true.

Guiding their sons through life is what daddys do,
but this adventure has been extra special because you're my best friend, too.

Walking through the door, I cannot wait to see your grin—
as we let each other know we are best friends to the end.

I look at your picture daily, remembering how we first met.
Time is beginning to take off like a jet.

Too soon you were ready to go to school, and I knew it was time,
but a part of me wanted to hold on to you and say, "No, you're all mine."

The first day of school came with emotions and cheers—
the day Daddy had feared for years was finally here.

When I picked you up, you came running, as happy as can be—
telling me all about the great adventures you'd had, and I replied, "I see."

You continued to tell me about all your new friends
and how you wished this day would never end.

Then with even more excitement, as I listened and smiled,
you said, "Daddy, I have a new best friend, and his name is Miles."

I gave you a great big hug like I always do
and said, "Listen to these words to hold on to:

COLOR THE IMAGE

FIND THE BALL

Made in the USA
Lexington, KY
28 January 2018